ONE MIND, ONE

A COLORING BOOK AND JOURNAL

BY MARY JANE MILLER

One Mind, One World

By Mary Jane Miller

Book and cover design by Mary M Meade

Illustrations by Emiliano Jimenez Ludekens

@Copyright Mary Jane Miller 2015 All rights reserved.

Permission for reproduction of this material by classroom teachers or instructor for use with students or home school, not commercial resale, is granted by virtue of purchase of this book. Such permission does not include storage of any part of this book in a retrieval system or the transmission of such, in any form, or by any means , electronic, mechanical, or otherwise without prior permission from the author, except as provided by USA copyright law.

First Printing: 2015

ISBN 978-1-312-86615-7

This original sketchbook of ideas and images for mediation, written or drawn is an offering for all ages. For children and adults, whether you're in the hospital, the church bible study or a member of the growing iconography community, this little resource has proven to be an asset for everyone on the path.

Websites:

peacebestill.net, millericons.com, sanmiguelicons.com, sacrediconretreat.com

Rejoice in our Diversity— An Ecumenical dialogue

Religious traditions around the globe have attempted to teach ordinary people to live and think about their existence. One Mind, One World was inspired by my art installation The Dialogue for Global Peace, a beautiful visual history, created for meditation encouraging believers to break free from what divides us. The art Installation aims at aligning our thinking with that of great religious leaders and philosophers, promoting peace on earth and the idea we are all one.

This book contains line drawing of the paintings from The Dialogue and represents a sampling of the holy, the mystical, the miraculous, and the forever impossible-possible, ideas from civilizations. Interfaith and peace education curriculum's might one day be required in every school at every level, as well as religious education and tolerance programs in every temple, ashram, church and mosque world-wide.

New age spirituality and ancient wisdom work together in this collection, aiming at highlighting the human search for divinity and the diversity we have shared. Looking over the images, noticing their purpose and historical dates hopefully will encourage some curiosity, to know more and understand what part of the archetypes live in you.

The subconscious is a repository of experiences which defines our behavior, likened to a "garden," in which thought, word and deed seeds are planted. The only way to cultivate a higher being is to go in the garden and see what is there. We are each our own gardener, exploring what we think as we go about the day. This coloring book invites you to explore your garden.

Every day we have an opportunity to be new, to adjust our visions and insights, to learn to conform to the idea of a safer and more beautiful world. Gardening is hard work, using something as simple as a coloring book may prove to be a way to dig out the old, nurture the new.

One Mind One World is a book, a memoir and offering, to document your knowledge of the world inside you and around you. The book has one objective: to ignite the question, "What do I know?" then listen and watch internally for the small burning flames of hope, joy, peace, charity, forgiveness, abundance, love, etc. and let that become a new meditation.

Our consciousness is changing. Are we willing to allow Jesus and the philosopher Lao Tzu, to be positioned beside the Mayan corn God and Buddha beside Mohammad? Use the Journal space to record what you "hear" and "receive" from coloring the images. In the process, recognize commonalities and your response. Ask questions and write as if the "answers" given becomes your memoir.

Peace be with you,

Mary Jane Miller

Atisha 980 AD

Every living being has the same basic wish – to be happy and to avoid suffering. Atisha is said to be the first Dali Lama of Tibet saying he would return in another form, here began the practice of looking for the next incarnation of the Dali Lama.

My reflections:

Many Faced Buddah 1200 BC

Many Faced Buddha also known as Phra Phrom in Thailand representation of the Hindu God Brahma who is regarded as the deity of good fortune and protection. In India the four faced Buddha Brahma is the God of creation, mercy and benevolence.

My reflections:

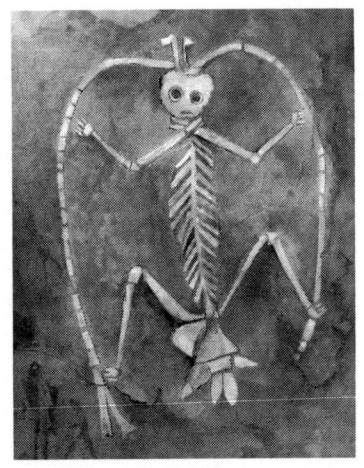

Australian Cave Painting 1200 BC

Aboriginal elders gathered in cave interiors to perform solemn rituals. Namarrkon, the Aboriginal Lightning spirit, lives above the clouds and is associated with intense electrical storms, illustrated with a circuit of lightning encircling its body.

My reflections:

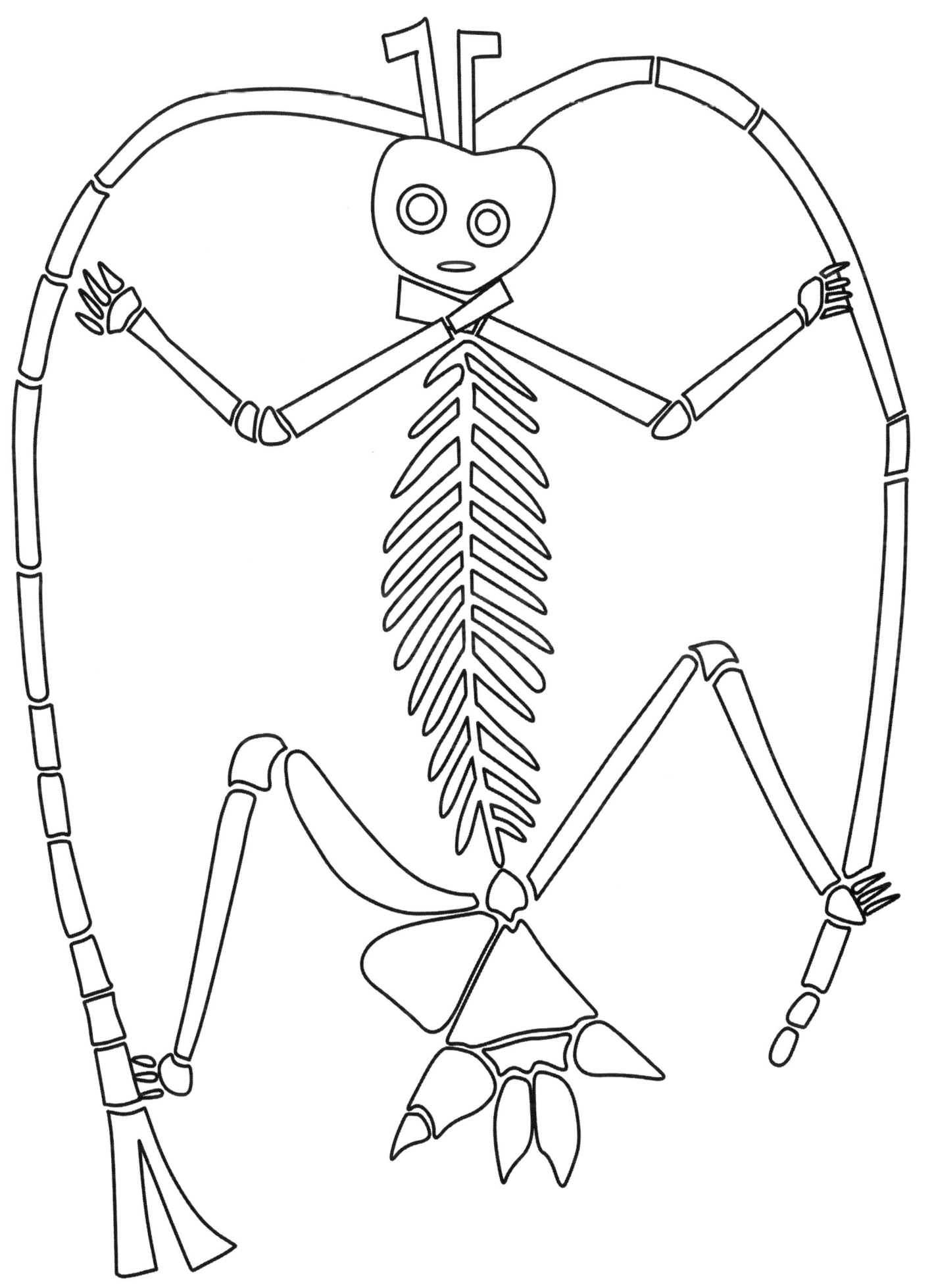

Buddah 600 bc

Siddhārtha Gautama was an ancient India spiritual teacher. "Buddha" meaning "awakened one" or "the enlightened one." His philosophy states, whatever problems we experience come from illusions in the mind.

My reflections:

___
___
___
___
___
___
___
___
___

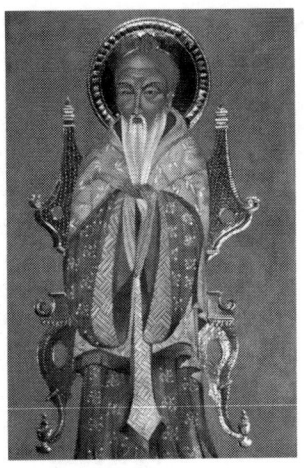

Confucius 551 BC

He was a Chinese philosopher who believed that the essential duties of human society required organization and agreement, even conformity. His teachings focused on creating ethical models for family and public interaction by setting educational standards.

My reflections:

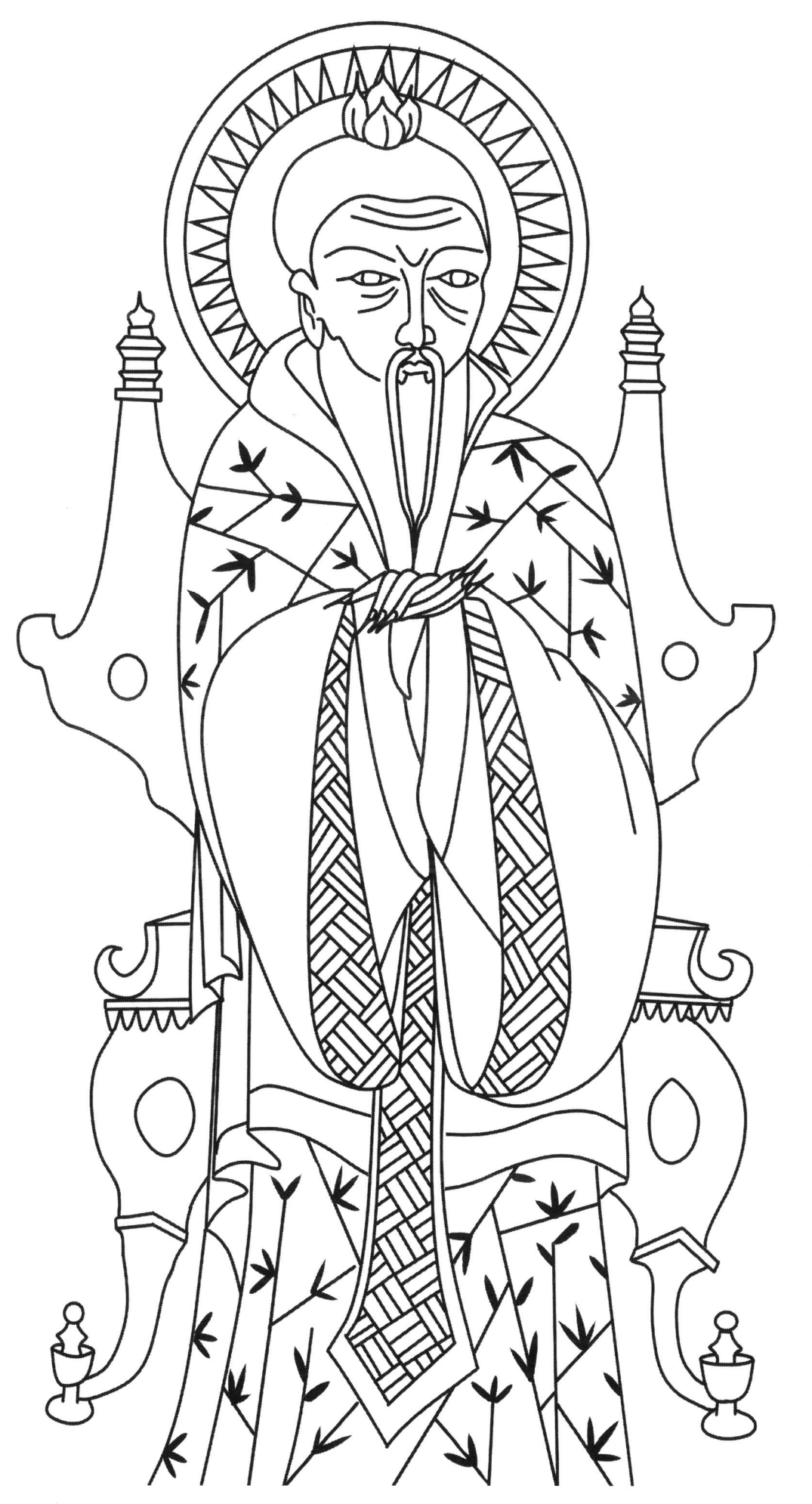

Christ 100 AD

Followers of Jesus Christ are known as Christians. "God became man that man might become God." "Love god with your whole heart and Love your neighbor as yourself." The name in Greek means "anointed" and in Hebrew the word means "messiah."

My reflections:

_____

_____

_____

_____

_____

_____

_____

_____

_____

_____

The image is taken for the relief found on the Gundestrup Cauldrons, in Denmark. The motifs and images surrounding these vessels draw the observer into an alien universe. Elephants, lions and several unknown gods, represent a foreign style, but what the intent of the message is still open to question.

My reflections:

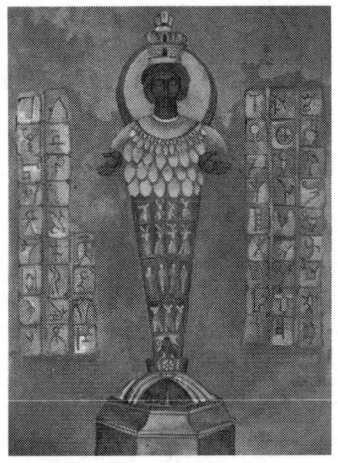

Diana 550BC

This heathen goddess was revered and admired as a "great" goddess; she symbolized the generative and nutritive powers of nature, and so was represented with many breasts. Her original temple was founded 580 BC.

My reflections:

_____

_____

_____

_____

_____

_____

_____

_____

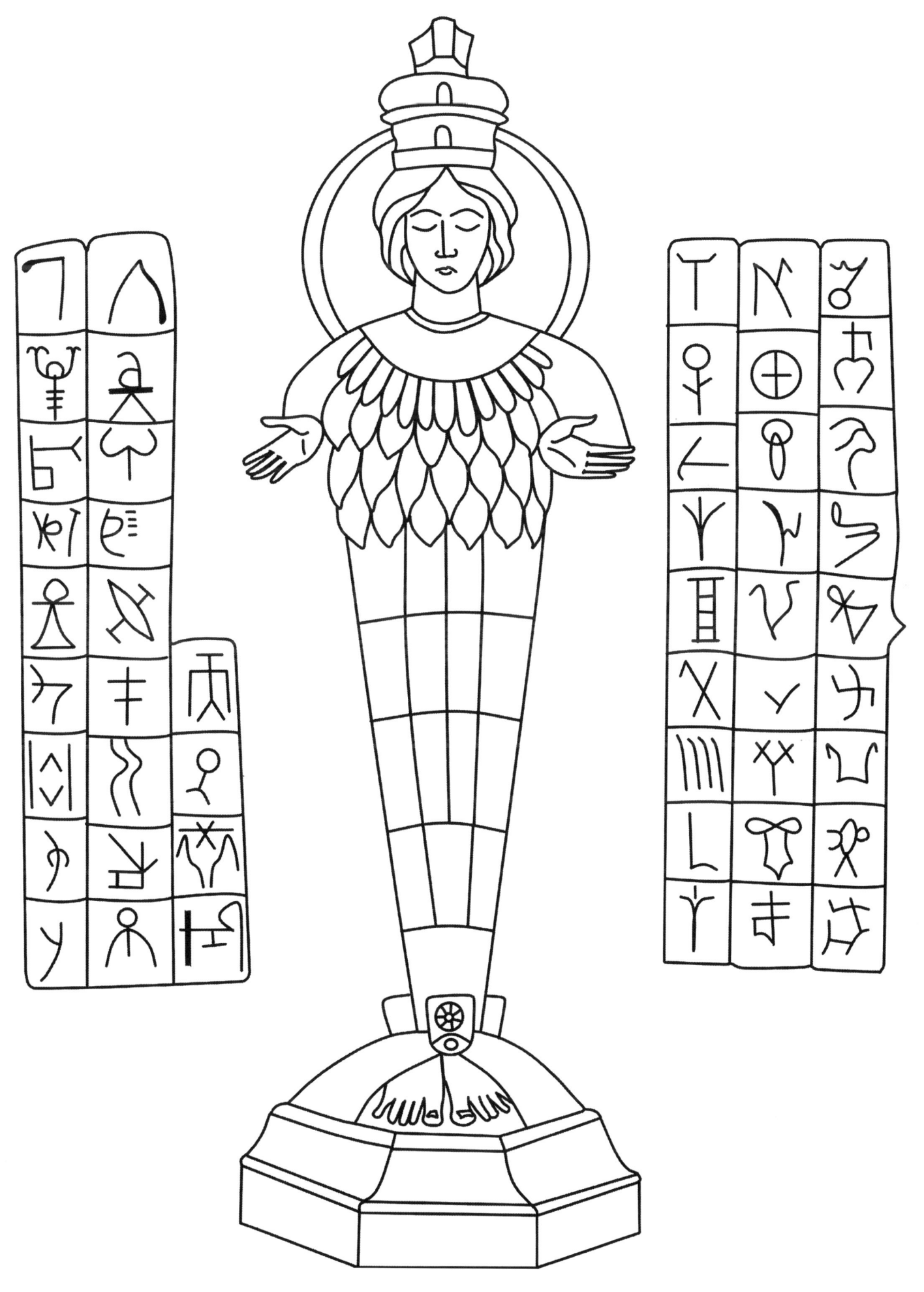

Corn God 30 AD

In Mayan mythology, Yum Caax ("lord of the woods") was the God of agriculture and nature, God of wild plants and animals summoned to protect the corn crop. The rainmaker God Chac is the protector of Yum Caax who rules the earth and its abundance.

My reflections:

Copernicus 1473 AD

Copernicus was a Polish astronomer and mathematician who radically changed mankind imagined perception of our Earth in orbit, it is not flat and not the center of the universe. This theory profoundly altered all the later astronomical views of the universe. His and Galileo's finding were so radical they were rejected by the Catholic Church.

My reflections:

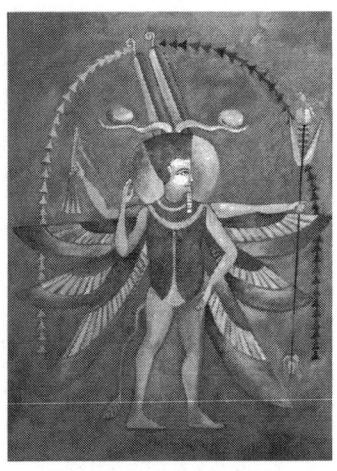

Glyph no date

No date because this is an invented image. It reflects multiple iconic symbols, elements common to many cultures past and present. The four corners, the eggs and energy radiating represent abundant life. It is not man, not insect, not known or worshiped.

My reflections:

Gilgamesh 2700 BC

King of Ur in Babylonia, on the River Euphrates in modern Iraq. Gilgamesh is depicted as a divine being of superhuman strength. Gilgamesh is strong and dominant defending the myth of the kingdom.

My reflections:

Ganesha 400 AD

One of the best-known and most widely worshiped deities in the Hindu pantheon. Ganesha is widely revered as the remover of obstacles, the patron of arts and sciences and the diva of intellect and wisdom.

My reflections:

Japan 700 BC

Ritual clay figurine utilized in mystic-religious rites, called Shakko-Dogu, they represent the invisible forces of nature and the universe. Very little is known about the culture. Thousands of these small figurines have been found all over Japan as well as under the water in its surrounding oceans.

My reflections:

Huehueteotl 500 AD

One of the oldest deities from ancient Aztec culture in America. Often depicted as an old man, indicating his great wisdom, he is shown wearing a large brazier marked with symbols of fire hence his name, Huehueteotl the "Fire God."

My reflections:

___

___

___

___

___

___

___

___

___

Incas Peru 950 AD

Viracocha is the great creator God, one of the most important deities in the Inca pantheon and seen as the creator of all things, or the substance from which all things are created, and intimately associated with the sea. Viracocha created the universe, sun, moon, and stars, time and civilization itself.

My reflections:

___
___
___
___
___
___
___
___
___

Lao Tzu 600 bc

Lao Tzu 600 BC Chinese Taoist Philosopher said "I have just three things to teach: simplicity, patience, compassion." He also said "if it is called the Tao it is not the Tao. To name God is to limit God".

My reflections:

___
___
___
___
___
___
___
___
___

Lilith 1778 BC

Perhaps originated in Iraq, Lilith the Queen of the night symbolizes the sun, flanked by owls, symbols of wisdom and perched upon a double lioness. Lilith was also named within the Hebrew tradition and is thought to have been Adam's first wife or a later descendant called Ishtar.

My reflections:

Mohammed 570 AD

Founder of the Islam religion, Mohammad is regarded by Muslims as their spiritual leader and prophet. By translating sacred text into Arabic he helped to integrate the many nomadic tribal languages. He also instituted singing to God in the form of chant five times a day.

My reflections:

Mother Teresa of Calcutta was entrusted with the mission of proclaiming God's thirsting love for humanity, especially for the poorest of the poor. She was awarded the Jewel of India, the highest honor bestowed on Indian civilians, and Soviet Union's Gold Medal of the Soviet Peace Committee. In 1979, she received the Nobel Peace Prize in recognition of her work "in bringing help to suffering humanity."

My reflections:

_____

_____

_____

_____

_____

_____

_____

_____

_____

_____

Pueblo Indian 1000 AD

Their name means "The People" or "Children of Holy People" a culture rich in ceremony and ritual. Native American Indians paint on the ground for ceremony, they are commonly called dry painting or sand painting. The ritual drew attention to the belief the images were "places where the gods come and go".

My reflections:

_____

_____

_____

_____

_____

_____

_____

_____

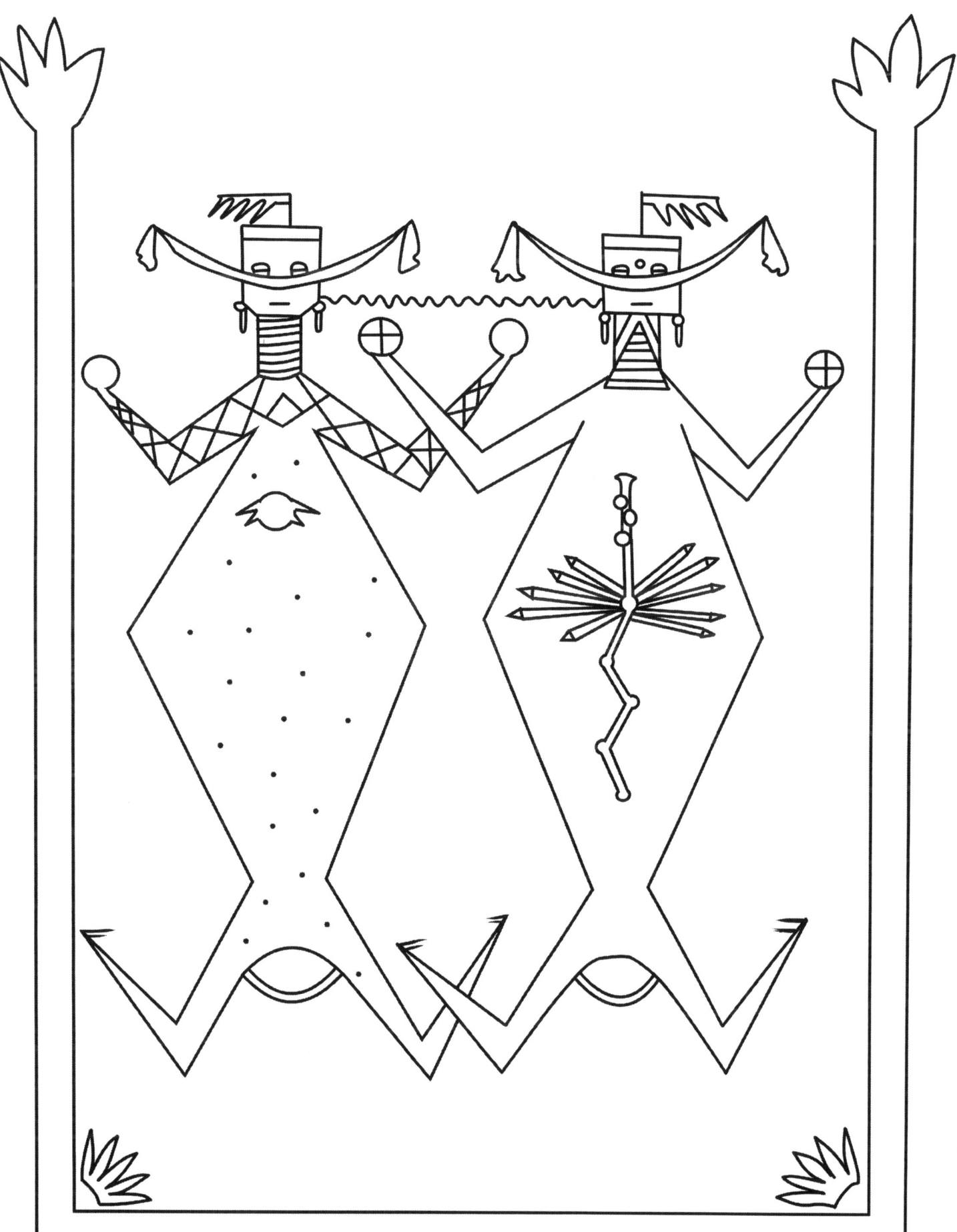

Moses 1200 BC

Hebrew prophet, liberator, leader, lawgiver, and historian, declaring that God is One. As a Young man he went up the mountain and heard the voice of God and as old man he received the tablets and the Law.

My reflections:

___
___
___
___
___
___
___
___
___

Nigeria 1000 BC

This fertility urn is from Central Nigeria's culture of Nok . They sculpted many grave markers and sacramental urns to prevent crop failure, infertility, and illness. Their culture though advanced, mysteriously vanished around 200 AD in the region of West Africa.

My reflections:

_____

_____

_____

_____

_____

_____

_____

_____

_____

Nefertiti and Horus 3000 BC

Nefertiti & God Horus 3000 BC Nefertiti stands hand and hand with the falcon headed Horus the Egyptian God of war, protection, and the sky. Nefertiti is one of the best known Egyptian queens, here depicted equal in size and structure to the God Horus.

My reflections:

_____

_____

_____

_____

_____

_____

_____

_____

_____

Sumerian 2600 BC

Akkadian, Assyrian, Sumerian and Amorites cultures sculpted these figurines; made from white gypsum with shells and black limestone for the eyes. These Mesopotamian sculptures were placed inside the temple to pray while the person who donated them went about their daily work.

My reflections:

_____

_____

_____

_____

_____

_____

_____

_____

_____

Plato 347 BC

One of the first Greek philosophers who understood that God comprises everything and at the same time exceeds everything. The mind is mans finest asset. He lived between the lives of Socrates and Aristotle. Aristotle suggested that Socrates' idea of forms can be discovered through investigation of the natural world, while Plato's idea of forms existed beyond and outside the ordinary range of human understanding.

My reflections:

Artist Statement

Interfaith dialogue is a contemporary idea behind One mind, One World attempting to connect us without losing our individual identity or respect for each other. There is a specific, qualitative difference between each image. Cultivating a dialogue with other religions and cultures brings about a deeper tolerance for every human and religious conviction. Mary Jane Miller continues to work towards this end within herself as well as through her art.

Copies of this book can be found on Lulu.com under Author Mary Jane Miller

Other books

In Light of Women her latest icon collection created as an exploration of women's image in iconography and their voices in the church. Vibrant text describing each images history, religious context and her own reflections about the world we live in today.

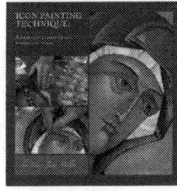

Icon Painting Technique, A Meditation and Guide to Egg Tempera explains the subtle relationship between the process of icon painting and how it reflects and enriches ones spiritual life. Mary Jane Miller discusses her technique, the history and meaning of icon painting.

Ancient image, Sacred Lines are icon templates for painting and drawing for adults and children alike. Each drawing is a meditation for healing or a template for iconographers. It is a tool for becoming more present in hope of softening the extreme moments of our lives. Grace comes when we least expect it. Color your world and celebrate your being here now.

The Mary Collection This collection of Mary icons captures the great mysteries of the Madonna, drawing attention to the relationship between Mary and Christ, and the viewer. A wide range of imagination and potential is explored this tiny book.

Check out her Websites:
peacebestill.net, millericons.com, sanmiguelicons.com, sacrediconretreat.com

Made in the USA
Lexington, KY
18 May 2018